THE

NONVIOLENCE

HANDBOOK

A Guide for Practical Action

MICHAEL N. NAGLER

BK·

Berrett–Koehler Publishers, Inc.
San Francisco
a BK Currents book

Berrett-Koehler Publishers, Inc.
235 Montgomery Street, Suite 650
San Francisco, CA 94104-2916
Tel: (415) 288-0260   Fax: (415) 362-2512   www.bkconnection.com

Ordering Information
Quantity sales. Special discounts are available on quantity purchases by corporations, associations, and others. For details, contact the "Special Sales Department" at the Berrett-Koehler address above.
Individual sales. Berrett-Koehler publications are available through most bookstores. They can also be ordered directly from Berrett-Koehler: Tel: (800) 929-2929; Fax: (802) 864-7626; www.bkconnection.com.
Orders for college textbook/course adoption use. Please contact Berrett-Koehler: Tel: (800) 929-2929; Fax: (802) 864-7626.
Orders by U.S. trade bookstores and wholesalers. Please contact Ingram Publisher Services, Tel: (800) 509-4887; Fax: (800) 838-1149; E-mail: customer .service@ingrampublisherservices.com; or visit www.ingrampublisherservices .com/Ordering for details about electronic ordering.

Berrett-Koehler and the BK logo are registered trademarks of Berrett-Koehler Publishers, Inc.

Printed in the United States of America
Berrett-Koehler books are printed on long-lasting acid-free paper. When it is available, we choose paper that has been manufactured by environmentally responsible processes. These may include using trees grown in sustainable forests, incorporating recycled paper, minimizing chlorine in bleaching, or recycling the energy produced at the paper mill.

Library of Congress Cataloging-in-Publication Data
Nagler, Michael N.
The nonviolence handbook : a guide for practical action / Michael N. Nagler.
— First edition.
    pages cm
Includes bibliographical references and index.
ISBN 978-1-62656-145-8 (pbk.)
1. Nonviolence. 2. Conflict management. I. Title.
HM1281.N343 2014
303.6'1--dc23
                    2013041434

First Edition
19 18 17 16 15 14   10 9 8 7 6 5 4 3 2 1

Interior design/art: Laura Lind Design   *Editor:* Todd Manza
Cover design: Kirk DouPonce   *Proofreader:* Henri Bensussen
Production service: Linda Jupiter Productions   *Indexer:* Linda Webster

For all those who have the faith that
humanity can be redeemed by nonviolence
and the courage to prove it.

*"Nonviolence is the greatest power humankind
has been endowed with."*

—Mahatma Gandhi

Contents

Foreword

I was honored when Professor Nagler approached me to write a foreword for this excellent book, both because of the book's timeliness—there is an urgent need for nonviolence in every possible application today—and because he is so eminently qualified to write it.

Over the past twelve years, we have seen the United States take military action to attempt to resolve political issues in Afghanistan, Iraq, Libya, Pakistan, Somalia, and Yemen. The disastrous results of those military actions underscore the value of a different approach to conflict resolution both nationally and internationally. Michael Nagler's manual on nonviolence is a healthy reminder that there are alternatives to violence.

I'm writing this foreword to *The Nonviolence Handbook* while on a trip in Northeast Asia. In two of the countries I've visited, citizens are using nonviolent tactics to challenge actions of their governments—the very situation on which Professor Nagler primarily focuses (though many others come under review). For instance, in Japan, where the war article of the Japanese constitution is under attack, Japanese citizens have formed Article 9 defense committees in every village and every suburb to rally support for the constitution that has successfully kept them out of wars and military actions since World War II.

In South Korea, Jeju Island is the site of a remarkable nonviolent struggle against the building of a naval
base for South Korean and American Aegis ballistic
missile defense systems. Here, for the past seven years,
the citizens of Gangjeong village have challenged their
government's destruction of a pristine marine area and
a mammoth, ancient lava rock formation for the construction of the naval base. They have used a variety of
tactics, including building peace camps on the remarkable rock formation called Gurumbei, forming human
blockades at base entrances, boarding barges transport-
ing huge concrete blocks intended for a breakwater on
unique coral heads, climbing and occupying huge construction cranes, and forming human chains of thousands of people around the base.

So far, these herculean nonviolent efforts have not
succeeded in stopping the construction of the naval
base. On the other hand, on the island of Okinawa,
where for the past twenty years citizens have challenged U.S. and Japanese government use of the island
for 75 percent of America's Japanese military presence,
their long protest has finally resulted in the process of
removing ten thousand U.S. military personnel from
the island.

Citizens around the world are looking for ways
to challenge harmful government policies and to address many other forms of injustice. *The Nonviolence
Handbook* points us toward those ways. Anyone who
can give us some pointers on practicing nonviolence
more safely and effectively is doing humankind a ser-

vice. But Professor Nagler is not just "anyone" in this field. His unusual expertise enables him to clearly explain the compelling, inspiring theory of nonviolence, its higher vision of humanity, and selected key episodes from its dramatic history. In the end we have, exactly as the subtitle suggests, a guide to the kind of action that the world so urgently needs.

I know courage when I see it, and I have seen more courage in the brave, determined citizens cited in Professor Nagler's examples—as well as those I myself have witnessed—than in the heavily armed forces arrayed against them. That courage, complemented by the knowledge of the skillful use of nonviolence, as provided in this handbook, is a recipe for a world of peace and justice. I hope that many people will use this book to help us build that world.

Ann Wright

Col. U.S. Army (Ret.)

Recipient, State Department Award for Heroism

one

An Introduction to Nonviolence

The twentieth century left us a double legacy. On the one hand, it was a time of great cruelty and violence; on the other hand, and perhaps from that very crucible of violence, we saw manifestations of a new kind of power—or rather, new uses of an age—old power—that can lead humanity to a far better future. In the years since Mahatma Gandhi demonstrated the power of nonviolence to free India from colonial rule and Martin Luther King Jr. employed it to liberate people of color from some of their oppression in the United States, countless peoples around the world—from Manila to Moscow, Cape Town to Cairo, and in the Occupy movements worldwide—have had varying degrees of success using one or another aspect of nonviolence to loosen the bonds of exploitation and oppression.

The practice of nonviolence touches on something fundamental about human nature, about who we wish to be as individuals or as a people. Gandhi stated simply, "Nonviolence is the law of our species."[1] Dr. Vandana Shiva, a renowned leader of rural resistance in India, said in a recent lecture that if we do not adopt nonviolence we risk compromising our humanity. Likewise, Iraqi Kurdish activist Aram Jamal Sabir said that although nonviolence may be harder and may require greater sacrifice than violence, "at least you don't lose your humanity in the process."[2]

We might contrast this with the appallingly high rates of depression, substance abuse, and suicide among today's American servicemen and women. As one of them told a documentary filmmaker, "I no longer like who I am. I lost my soul in Iraq." Another told a friend of mine, who was on his way to the Middle East as part of a Christian Peacemaker team, "I am still haunted by the things we did . . . I would give anything to be able to go back and undo some of the things we did. But I can't. But at least I can thank you with all my heart for doing what you do." Through these words, which are a testimony to human nature, we glimpse both the costs of violating that aspect of our nature and the path toward its redemption.

It is not surprising, therefore, that here and there the significance of nonviolence has begun to be recognized by people looking for a new story of human nature and human destiny, who find themselves searching for a badly needed higher image of humanity. Frankly, our present worldview and the institutions based on that worldview take violence as a norm, and shifting that basis could lead to a leap forward in cultural evolution. It could resolve or show us how to resolve our economic, environmental, personal, and international problems. In short, the full recognition of nonviolence could rewrite the story of human destiny.

However, at this time most people do not understand the dynamics of nonviolence fully, if at all. Few people know its potential or exactly how to use it to liberate themselves and all of us from greed, tyranny, and injustice. Nonviolence may be embedded in our nature, as Gandhi said, but it cannot emerge into our lives and institutions until it is much better understood. Episodes of nonviolence are constantly cropping up, but to use it safely and effectively—and certainly to use it for lasting change—requires knowledge and planning.

Fight, Flight, and the Third Way

Nonviolence seems to be rare, even the exception, and its potential—perhaps even its mere possibility—is rigorously ignored by policy makers. Violence, or deliberate harm to another's person or basic dignity, is so common as to seem ubiquitous, especially when we include, as we should, structural violence—

the exploitation or dominance built into a system. But the seeming ubiquity of violence and rarity of nonviolence turns out to have more to do with the way we see the world than with the way the world really is. The way we practiced science until the twentieth century, for instance, tended to emphasize materialism, separateness, and competition, leading to the image of "nature red in tooth and claw." It is only recently that science has undergone a remarkable shift toward a more balanced vision not only of human nature but also of nature and evolution in general. This development has the greatest significance for nonviolence but has yet to make its way into the prevailing worldview.[3]

Another reason we are not more aware of instances of nonviolence, and the reason it all too often seems ineffectual or to end up with a disappointing sequel, as in Egypt and Syria, is that modern culture does not prepare us very well to understand a positive, nonmaterial force. Indeed, the word *nonviolence* itself is part of the problem. *Non*-violence implies that the real something, the default condition, is violence, and that nonviolence is just its absence—in the same way that many people still think of peace as merely the absence of war. They are turning truth on its head, and artificially limiting our options.

If we are unaware of nonviolence, we will tend to believe that our only response to an attack is to give in or to fight back—the fight-or-flight response. From the perspective of nonviolence, this is really no choice at all. Either approach—passively allowing violence to be used against us (or, for that matter, someone else) or reacting in kind—will only serve to increase the violence. Our real choice is not between these two expressions of violence; instead, it's the choice that opens when we don't want to take either approach. Then we want to confront violence with an alternative, with what Andrew Young, citing an old spiritual, called a "way out of no way."[4]

Nonviolence offers us a viable, natural third way out of the fight-or-flight conundrum. The twentieth-century discoveries of relativity and quantum reality showed us that nothing is as separate as it seems. Similarly, there is now a good deal of evidence that empathy and cooperation are in fact the dominant forces in evolution, that human beings and other primates are equipped with "mirror neurons" that enable us to share what another is feeling, that self-sacrifice can produce intense rewards in the nervous system—and, of course, that nonviolence is an extremely effective tool for social change.[5]

Natural as nonviolence may be, however, there is no denying that empathy and care for the well-being of someone who's against us do not come easily. It can be quite a struggle, but it's encouraging to remember that this very struggle is the source of nonviolent power. As King put it, "The phrase 'passive resistance' often gives the false impression that this is a sort of 'do-nothing method' in which the resister quietly and passively accepts evil. But nothing is further from the truth. For while the nonviolent resister is passive in the sense that he is not physically aggressive toward his opponent, his mind and emotions are always active, constantly seeking to persuade his opponent that he is wrong."[6]

To be angry at injustice and to fear harm are natural human responses. The point is not whether we have the "right" to be frightened or outraged but how we can use that fear or outrage to change a situation most effectively. As a preeminent nonviolence scholar, Gene Sharp, has pointed out, the first thing an oppressed people must do is to overcome the paralyzing fear that has kept them down.[7] In Chile, for instance, constitutional means were enough to bring down Augusto Pinochet in 1989 and to end the nation's long nightmare of military rule, but first they had to overcome their fear, which gave them the creative power for action.

No doubt we will have to undergo this personal struggle against our "natural" feelings many times, but it does eventually become a habit. And when we can express our fear or anger as creative energy, the creative power of nonviolence is in our hands. Emotionally, we are neither running away in fear nor attacking in anger; we are resisting in love. In terms of our conscious intention, we are neither looking to "win" nor afraid of losing; our aim is to grow, if possible, even along with those opposing us.

The Uses of Nonviolence

We have all used nonviolent energy countless times in countless interactions, without naming it as such. We catch ourselves on the point of making a sharp criticism of someone and think, "Well, I guess I've done that too, sometimes," and say something kind instead. We swallow our impatience when the guy in front of us in line takes too much time. A friend of mine, to escalate our examples, shook hands with a would-be carjacker, asked the startled young man if he needed some money, and sent him on his way.

Nonviolence, as a fundamental energy, is quietly operating at all times, like gravity. We tend to use the term *nonviolence* only when some kind of conflict erupts, especially between a people and their government, but the thing itself is working unnoticed in many other areas and can be used in any situation, from national revolutions to personal interactions. Therefore, although my examples in this book mainly focus on people who find themselves in an insurrectionary movement, all of us can benefit from understanding the dynamics of this force. Anyone who is confronted by one of the many forms of violence in our world (whether this is outright force or an inequity built into a system) and feels called upon to assert his or her human dignity against that violence can benefit from taking a nonviolent stance toward all living things. My hope is that this book, in conjunction with the various resources listed in the back, can help activists understand the main principles underlying the dynamics of nonviolent action, but with a little imagination anyone can use these principles in their daily life. They can become our way of life. Such a turn toward nonviolence first requires that we outgrow our present image of ourselves as separate, physical, and competitive. Imagine if we were to seek out a third way in international relations, in deplorable situations such as Rwanda or Syria, for instance, when the international community thinks its only options are to bomb someone (fight) or to do nothing (flight). A whole array of very different options would open up if enlightened state actors understood what nonviolence really is: international law, good offices and diplomacy, reconciliation commissions, and so forth. Nonstate or civil society actors could do even more—such as third-party nonviolent interventions—and they are beginning to realize this.

There is no quick and easy way to become nonviolent. It calls for constant effort and becomes a lifelong challenge. Learning about it is very helpful, but this is only a beginning. Learning *along with practice* is much more effective.

Fortunately, nonviolence offers many ways to create permanent, long-term positive changes that would enable us to rebuild social institutions on a more humane and sustainable basis. Not all of those approaches need to be confrontational, as we will see. Each of us, whatever our station in life or relation to activism, can carry out this grand "experiment with truth," to paraphrase Gandhi, according to our own capacities and the situations we confront.

Because the principle or energy of nonviolence can be applied in different ways by different practitioners and in so many different situations, I have concentrated here on the principle or energy itself, without trying to spell out very often just how it can best be applied. With a good infrastructure and a little imagination we can adapt the principle to any given situation, and of course work out best practices of our own, when the basic principles are assimilated.[8]

Satyagraha: A New Term for an Eternal Principle

Reading "history" might give you the impression that life unfolds in an endless series of competitions, conflicts, and wars. But as far back as 1909, Gandhi pointed out that history as we have practiced it is "a record of every interruption of the even working of the force of love or the soul. . . . Soul-force, being natural, is not noted in history."[9] Note that Gandhi does not use the word *nonviolence* here, which had not yet become current (as a translation of *ahimsa*), and he had rejected the misleading term "passive resistance." Around this period he had to invent another term, *satyagraha* (pronounced sat-YAH-gra-ha), which literally means "clinging to truth." Satyagraha is sometimes used to mean nonviolence in general, as in this quote, but sometimes it means nonviolence in the form of active, resistant struggle.

By coining the term *satyagraha*, based on the Sanskrit word *sat*, which means "truth" or "reality" (as well as "the good"), Gandhi made it quite clear that he saw nonviolence as the positive reality of which violence is the shadow or negation. Consequently, nonviolence was bound to prevail in the long run: "The world rests upon the bedrock of *satya* or truth. *Asatya*, meaning untruth, also means nonexistent, and *satya* or truth also means that which is. If untruth does not so much as exist, its victory is out of the question. And truth being that which is, can never be destroyed. This is the doctrine of satyagraha in a nutshell."[10]

Though *satyagraha* literally means "clinging to truth," it is often translated, not inappropriately, as "soul force." We all have that force within us, and under the right circumstances it can come forth from anyone, with amazing results. This can best be seen in what's called a *nonviolent moment*, when the "unstoppable force" of one party's nonviolence confronts the apparently immoveable commitment to violence of another. This moment will always lead to success, sometimes evidently and immediately, sometimes further down the road.

For instance, in 1963 in Birmingham, Alabama, black marchers, inspired by the intention to "win our freedom, and as we do it . . . set our white brothers free," in the words of one of their leaders, found themselves unexpectedly blocked by a line of police and firemen with dogs and hoses. The marchers knelt to pray. After a while they became "spiritually intoxicated," as

David Dellinger recounts. They got up off their knees as though someone had given a signal and steadily marched toward the police and firemen. Once they got within earshot, some of them said, "We're not turning back. We haven't done anything wrong. All we want is our freedom. How do you feel doing these things?"[11] Even though the police commissioner, a notorious segregationist, repeatedly shouted, "Turn on the hoses!" the firemen found their hands frozen. The marchers walked steadily on, passing right through the lines of the police and firemen. Some of these men were seen to be crying.

Gandhi, who had seen this working time and again, gave a beautiful explanation of how this transformation takes place: "What satyagraha does in these cases is not to suppress reason but to free it from inertia and to establish its sovereignty over prejudice, hatred, and other baser passions. In other words, if one may paradoxically put it, it does not enslave, it compels reason to be free." What he calls "reason" here is better described as the innate awareness that we are all connected and that nonviolence is "the law of our species." As we've noted, this is an awareness latent in everyone, a natural human state, however temporarily obscured it may be by the fog of hatred. In principle, we should be able to awaken this awareness in virtually anyone, given enough time and know-how. Once awake, such awareness automatically takes precedence over the "baser passions."

That human beings have the potential to be non-violent—and to respond to nonviolence when it's offered—implies a much higher image of the human being than we are presented with in the mass media and throughout our present culture, but because of that very culture, we can't expect our nonviolent potential to manifest by itself. To bring it to fruition we must first try to understand it better and get into the habit of using it creatively in our relationships, our institutions, and our culture. Then, to use it in situations of intense conflict such as Birmingham, there are two basic ingredients that make the nonviolent magic work:

1. We approach our situation with right intention. We are not and do not need to be against the well-being of any person.

2. We employ right means. Wrong means such as violence can never, in the long run, bring about right ends.

The source of our empowerment and strength in satyagraha lies in our having right intention and using right means. If we operate from anger or envy or ignorance, then no matter how good the cause, we are not approaching it correctly. Note that the Birmingham marchers asked, "How do you feel doing this?" In other words, they credited the opponent with some moral awareness and thereby helped to awaken that awareness—for the opponent's own benefit.

Likewise, obviously, if we give in to violence, we are not employing right means. Let's look into each of these guidelines in turn.

two

Right Intention: Cultivating a Nonviolent Soul

The scriptures of all the world's faith traditions uphold "the fundamental unity of the human family on Earth," in the words of the 1993 Parliament of the World's Religions.[12] It is not surprising, then, that the best-known nonviolent leaders—Aung San Suu Kyi, Khan Abdul Ghaffar Khan, King, and of course Gandhi—drew upon their respective faiths for inspiration. Often, too, they drew on the spiritual practices within those faiths for the strength to see and to act nonviolently in the face of threats or abuse.

Whether we have a religious affiliation or not (and today we often do not), accessing the deeper resources of nonviolence requires some inkling that we are, in

King's words from the Birmingham jail, "tied in a single garment of destiny." There must be some sense of unity even with our opponents, some confidence that they can be reached, no matter how hostile their present state of mind. We must know that we have inner resources that make reliance on weapons, numbers, or money unnecessary and that there is a meaningful pattern to existence, such that every problem can be solved without essential harm to anyone.

The Person Is Not the Problem

In a nonviolent outlook, the "way out of no way," we no longer think of a dispute as a zero-sum game where, in order for me to win, you have to lose. It is not me against you but you and me against the problem; there is a way both of us can benefit and even grow. This ability to turn an argument into a problem-solving session, a dispute into a learning experience, and eventually a feeling of alienation into an awareness of unity benefits all parties and creates a strong attractor toward creative resolution for all. This is why it is so important for a nonviolent actor, who tries never to lose sight of the possibility of reconciliation, to "liquidate antagonism, not the antagonist."[13] Never be against people but only against problems.

It is not always easy to cultivate this intention, but there is a particularly useful way to make it work: we must try never to humiliate or to accept humiliation, for that hurts everyone. It is extremely difficult for anyone to live with shame or humiliation, and when someone threatens us with violence he or she does feel a little tug of shame for using that method, even if not consciously. When we offer to shift the ground of the conversation toward nonviolence, therefore, we are giving our counterpart a way out. This intention is acknowledged in one of the best terms for nonviolence that I know of in any language, *alay dangal,* or "to offer dignity," which was coined during the Philippines People Power Revolution of 1986.

Likewise, the Prophet Muhammad once told his followers that they must help everyone, even an oppressor. When they asked him how one can help an oppressor, he replied, "By preventing him from his oppression."[14] This gives us an extremely useful guideline to have in the forefront of our minds: The more you respect the humanity of your opponent, the more effectively you can oppose his or her injustice.

Thankfully, in satyagraha we are not forced to choose between the principled thing and the strategic thing to do; in the long run, the right means (like nonviolence) will bring about right ends (like justice). This brings up a really eye-opening feature of nonviolence. In contrast to, say, a military campaign, the basic resource that nonviolence draws upon is *unlimited.* When I give you respect, I don't give it away or reduce my own supply. Violence, on the other hand, focuses us on material things that are scarce and impermanent, creating a sense of competition and fear.

Our intention to separate people from problem, to maintain another's dignity along with our own, is both the method and the goal of satyagraha. As Gandhi said, "Real noncooperation is noncooperation with evil, and not with the evildoer," and he held onto this distinction even in the face of the hardest test nonviolence can face: defending a country against full-scale invasion by a determined enemy. In 1942, when India, her hands tied by the British, feared invasion by Japanese armies, he indicated how this could be done:

> If we were a free country, things could be done nonviolently to prevent the Japanese from entering the country. As it is, nonviolent resistance could commence the moment the Japanese effect a landing. Thus, nonviolent resisters would refuse them any help, even water. For it is no part of their duty to help anyone to steal their country. But if a Japanese had missed his way and was dying of thirst and sought help as a human being, a nonviolent resister, who may not regard anyone as his enemy, would give water to the thirsty one. Suppose the Japanese compel resisters to give them water, the resisters must die in the act of resistance.[15]

This bold vision became a reality when Soviet troops invaded Czechoslovakia to suppress reforms in 1968. Knowing that armed resistance would be futile, the resourceful Czechs courageously disobeyed curfews and all kinds of orders, but they fraternized with the Soviet soldiers and tried not to harbor anger toward them as people. As a result of this unexpected response, three Warsaw Pact armies totaling half a million troops were unable to gain control of the country for eight long months. Along with the Czech citizens' courage and sense of humor, it was their skill in separating people from policy, or evil from evildoer, that gave them a large measure of success against overwhelming odds. Today we call this strategy civilian-based defense, which along with unarmed civilian peacekeeping, forms the nonviolent equivalent to military defense.

Because all violence begins in the failure or refusal to recognize another as fully human, the deeper reaches of nonviolence must involve (re)awakening the humanity of one's opponent. Even a torturer, hard as it may be to remember, is a person—a person who, through ignorance and insensitivity, thinks it appropriate to torture another, but still, down in there somewhere, a person. Thus, even someone so dehumanized as to do such a thing has a hidden desire to be human again. We're appealing to this desire when we keep the personhood of the other in view, and this is why nonviolent resistance has been known to win over even heavily armed, highly determined opposition.[16] At the very least, nonviolence protects us from the corrosive effects of harboring anger and dehumanization. Let us not forget that our own personal freedom from anger, fear, and so forth is no small benefit of the practice of nonviolence.

An important element of our intention to treat an attacker as a human being is to avoid labeling him or her. Labels depersonalize, which is why soldiers so often use them to get over the natural psychological abhorrence we all feel at killing another. A truly nonviolent person will never depersonalize, humiliate, or dehumanize another, even—or especially—when resisting. What King said about injustice—that injustice anywhere is a threat to justice everywhere—applies equally to our dignity: degrading anyone degrades everyone. Going even further, we should actually work toward friendship and reconciliation, in the understanding that, as Abraham Lincoln said, "The best way to destroy an enemy is to make him a friend."

Five Basic Training Practices for Nonviolent Living

The temptation to shame someone who's behaving badly—that is, to try to make them ashamed of themselves rather than ashamed of what they're doing—can be very strong. Giving dignity to someone like that, acknowledging that they have a point of view, does not come naturally. But the attitude can be cultivated. Here are some elements of a nonviolent training program by which we can empower ourselves as individuals and cultivate right intention.[17]

1. *Avoid the major networks and media outlets.* Whether we realize it or not (because it has grown up gradually), mass media today are saturated with violence and with the low image of humanity violence implies.

Innumerable studies have shown that this violent imagery gets into our minds, even if we consciously disapprove, and makes us markedly more violent and aggressive. Normalizing the media would require a major campaign. Fortunately, there are alternative media today through which we can get news and entertainment (some are listed at the end of this book). Through them we are less likely to see the world as a violent place and ourselves as helpless to change it. We can safely reduce our exposure to the commercial mass media, beholden to corporate and power-structure interests—even to zero.

2. *Learn about nonviolence.* To fill the space left when we avoid such media, nothing is better than a greater appreciation and knowledge of nonviolence, which, as we have seen, is no mere technique but embodies in itself a worldview, an entire culture. Simply learning to spot the nonviolence happening around us is quite helpful. Formal learning, such as reading books like this and the others listed in our bibliography, adds another dimension. And a final potent means of gaining nonviolent culture is to practice it mindfully.

3. *Take up a spiritual practice* if you do not already have one. Meditation, which need not be connected with a particular religion, is extremely helpful for the nonviolent—or for anyone.[18] Meditation is a great humanizer because it puts us in touch with the deeper reaches of our own humanity, which is simultaneously that of others. We all need some form of self-

discipline, whether religiously sanctioned or not, and many nonviolent actors today have gotten access to their inner resources and vision through meditation, prayer, or some other spiritual practice.

4. *Be more personal with others.* Throughout your daily interactions, give people your undivided attention. Take the trouble to chat with the toll collector (if there's not a long line of cars behind you); call someone up instead of texting—or better yet, go have tea with them. Use technology to connect with people rather than to distance yourself from them. These seemingly small habits can change the texture of our lives, helping us to develop compassion and see the humanity in others while, of course, helping them as well.

5. *Find a project and get active.* What is your unique contribution? Where does the world need you most? What project do you see as doable and critical to making an essential change in our present system? Quite a few studies have shown that those who are active are more optimistic and vice versa. We influence ourselves very much by what we do, perhaps as much or more than we influence ourselves by how we articulate why we're doing it.

These steps help to prepare us for nonviolent living. Even without Step 5 they would make a difference in the world, because how we live affects the world around us even if we do nothing else. But we will do something else.

three

Right Means: Knowing Where We Stand

When the popular Vietnamese Buddhist teacher Thich Nhat Hanh was asked to explain his concept of "Engaged Buddhism," he replied, "Engaged Buddhism is just Buddhism."[19] You cannot be true to spiritual values today without working actively to express those values in our unpeaceful world. However, although it's good to keep in mind that the values themselves are a good push in the right direction, we need to steer our subsequent actions like skilled pilots who know the dangers of the conflict terrain and know *how* to mobilize the strengths of nonviolence to meet them.

When should we use nonviolence, and in what forms? This is the question we should consider next.

How Much Nonviolence Is Enough?

Conflicts escalate when they are not resolved, and if they are left untended they can rapidly get out of control. From the nonviolence point of view, the intensity of a conflict is not necessarily a question of how many guns or how many people are involved (the same metric would work for a quarrel between lovers as between nations); it is primarily about how far dehumanization has proceeded. If someone no longer listens to you, is calling you names or is labeling you, it's probably too late for petitions.

In terms of knowing how to respond, we can conveniently think of this escalation in three stages that call for distinct sets of responses. Let's call these three stages Conflict Resolution, Satyagraha (active nonviolent resistance), and—hopefully this is rare, but it helps to know it exists—Ultimate Sacrifice (see Figure).

Stage 1: Conflict Resolution. It would be lovely to respond to every conflict early, when there is no serious dehumanization in the atmosphere. Here differences can be resolved using the well-known tools of conflict resolution or nonviolent communication. If you register a complaint, the other side will at least listen; they may not like you, but they're still aware that you are people. The tools that work at Stage 1, such as negotiation, mediation, and arbitration, sometimes with the

The Three Stages of Conflict Escalation

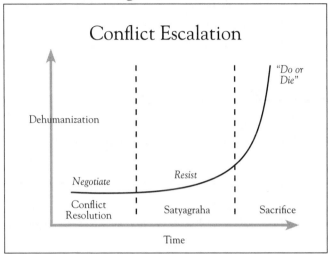

good offices of a third party, are relatively well-known and do not require much explication here.

Stage 2: Satyagraha. As we all know, however, conflicts are not always so manageable. There are times (pretty often, actually) when those whom we would persuade are not reachable through reason. This is when satyagraha comes into its own. It often means being willing to take on some suffering instead of dishing it out to others, in order to awaken them. As Gandhi put it, "Things of fundamental importance to the people are not secured by reason alone but have to be purchased with their suffering. . . . If you want something really important to be done you must not merely satisfy the reason, you must move the heart also."[20]

Gandhi actually refers to this as the "law of suffering." Suffering—whether it's standing up to physical abuse or renouncing an amenity or whatever—is a critical part of nonviolent persuasion in more serious conflicts.

Stage 3: The Ultimate Sacrifice. Stage 3 is really an extension of Stage 2, but here things have reached a life-or-death intensity. We've tried the usual techniques of satyagraha—strikes, defiance of orders, civil disobedience, and so on—but our "conversation partner," our opponent, is not responding (at least not visibly). However, we are still not without recourse on the nonviolent path. If we cannot live with an injustice, we can risk our lives to correct it. I have chosen those words carefully. It is not dying that can awaken a stubborn opponent so much as being *willing to risk* dying. This was the case in the do-or-die moment during the final stage of the Indian freedom struggle, for example, and it worked.

There are two things to bear in mind here. First, nonviolence is on the whole much safer than violence. Virtually no one has died in the act of unarmed civilian peacekeeping, for example, while millions died using the "normal" methods of armed struggle or war. Second, if we go into nonviolence *because* it's safer, that seems to rob it of some of its power. The full power of nonviolence comes when we do it because we believe it's right and we're not counting the cost.

Clearly, as the escalation curve in our figure indicates, the sooner we can take action in a conflict, the more options we have and the less pain we'll have to endure in resolving it. But we don't always have that choice. There is so much violence in the media (at least in the industrialized world) and our concept of human potential is correspondingly so low that conflicts can quickly spin out of control. We can't afford to ignore cases that require the most courageous response.

When Nothing Else Will Work

When an opponent has become so alienated that even well-executed satyagraha cannot awaken his conscience (at least not noticeably), yet the evil cannot be tolerated, *satyagrahis* (nonviolent actors) have often decided to risk making the ultimate sacrifice. In so doing, they have found themselves wielding the ultimate power in soul force, and much of the time—though not always—they have lived to tell the tale.

Consider my friend David Hartsough, now a famous peace activist, then a fifteen-year-old white person sitting in at a lunch counter in Virginia to break racial discrimination. After a day and a half without food he was suddenly pulled off his stool and threatened by an enraged white man who held a huge knife to his chest and snarled, "Well, n------lover, you have one minute to get out before I run this into your heart." David stayed calm (he had been reciting the Lord's Prayer to himself for hours on end). Trying to meet the man's eyes despite the hatred in them, he heard himself saying, "Brother, you do what you feel you have to, but I'm going to try to love you no matter what." After a long moment, the knife began to tremble. Then the man slowly dropped his hand and walked out of the lunchroom. Some onlookers noticed that he was in tears.

Remember, soldiers go into battle by the millions, fully prepared to risk their lives, often enough for dubious causes; must we not be ready to do as much? Our courage will have far greater transformative power than armed force, coming as it does from an unarmed person who is willing to risk harm but not inflict it. This is sometimes called the "power of vulnerability." As mentioned, far fewer people have been killed in the practice of active nonviolence than have been killed in armed struggles. Even so, we cannot avoid it altogether in serious conflicts—a good enough reason for using nonviolence at earlier stages of a conflict, if at all possible!

four

Putting Nonviolent Energy to Work

There are infinite creative ways to employ nonviolent energy, and although all of them grow out of
the principle that we should not and need not be
against the true well-being of anyone—our real needs
are never in conflict—some of the means that are best
employed may not be obvious. We have seen, for example, that right means must always be proportional; that
is, we must match violence with an equivalent nonviolent force, appropriate to the situation. Right means
also includes the art of compromise, which requires
an understanding of which principles are negotiable
and which are nonnegotiable. Finally, we must have
in mind specific goals and must understand how we

intend to meet those goals. In the end, keeping these principles in mind will help ensure that we have built our nonviolent movement right, from the ground up.

Proportionality

The social force of nonviolence must be applied in proportion to the degree of hostility it is facing. To take full advantage of the power of right means, therefore, we need to know which of the three stages we are at within a given conflict. Overreacting at the beginning of a struggle—for example, undertaking a fast, which is one of the most drastic steps in satyagraha, before giving our opponent a chance to be persuaded—can be as ineffective as continuing to protest when things have gone past the point where a protest will have the desired effect.

That conflicts can escalate is a matter of all-too-common experience. The part we don't often recognize is that nonviolence can escalate too. As King said in his 1967 Christmas Sermon on Peace, "We shall match your capacity to inflict suffering by our capacity to endure suffering." The degree of soul force should match the degree of threat force, or dehumanization. For instance, the run-up to the Iraq War in March 2003 brought millions of people around the world into the streets in vehement protest. When President George W. Bush airily dismissed protesters as a "focus group" he was in effect signaling that the disagreement had reached Stage 2: time for satyagraha.

It's not that the protests and petitions were wrong. We certainly should undertake good faith negotiations, even if we doubt our opponent will respond. It increases the legitimacy of our campaign, putting us in a stronger position to resist if and when that is needed, while also encouraging some rehumanization that will bear fruit in the long run. But we also must be ready to take concrete actions when it's clear that our opponent isn't listening.

The Art of Compromise

In anything from running a business to planning an economy it's important to distinguish goals from strategies. This is especially crucial in satyagraha because we want to retain the ability to compromise as much as possible. Therefore, we must identify basic principles that we cannot sacrifice for any reason—such as truth, human dignity, and freedom—and distinguish these from things that are negotiable, such as who gets credit for what. Often, when we find we're unwilling to compromise, it's because we're caught up in symbols—marches that go from one arbitrary place to another, ribbons of a particular color—which can turn an otherwise manageable situation into a power struggle, whether against our opponent or within our own ranks.

During an Occupy demonstration in Philadelphia in 2011, for instance, protesters were approached by representatives of the city's prestigious black churches, who wanted to join the movement and asked only that the protesters refrain from using certain obscenities in public. Unfortunately, the protesters refused to make this compromise. They confused a tactic—or really just a personal desire to curse in public—with their overall goal of securing economic justice, clinging to what should have been negotiable and thus failing to secure potentially powerful allies for their movement.

We must always remind ourselves that we are not engaged in a power struggle, whatever the other side may think, but in a learning process that has the potential to benefit everyone. Our ultimate goal, if it's at all possible, is to rebuild relationships. Most of all, remembering that there really is no conflict but only shared needs will help us to prioritize and to keep our eyes on the prize that's most important to all parties.

For instance, the first project of the great Italian activist Danilo Dolci, who gave up his lucrative career as an architect in Milan to work with the poor in Sicily, was to build a dam near the town of Jatto, much against the will of the Sicilian Mafia. Despite the opposition, Dolci succeeded. When a Mafioso came to him and grudgingly conceded, "Well, Danilo, you won. Now you get all the water," Dolci replied, "No, *we* have won. The water will be for you and your families, too."

In keeping with this attitude, Gandhi tried to observe what he called a principle of "non-embarrassment." When your opponent is preoccupied, as the South African government was preoccupied by a railroad strike in 1913, you back off. Gandhi's surprise introduction of common courtesy had an electrifying effect on his relationship with the government, and his willingness to compromise in this way was probably instrumental in the success of the eight-year satyagraha he waged for the Indian community's rights in that region. Always learning from his own experiences, he did the same thing nearly thirty years later when the British were preoccupied with World War II—again to very good effect.

What Do We Really Want?

Gandhi mastered the art of compromise to such an extent that his own people were often alarmed that he was giving away the store. They didn't understand that his willingness to concede everything else was what was helping them gain their main point—India's freedom—and that he was merely distinguishing overall goals from immediate strategies. In 1925, for instance, he was released from a long prison sentence, only to find that his party had suffered a serious division during his absence. The group opposing his position on an important issue now held the reins. Since they had won by fair means, Gandhi did not try to block them. Instead, he yielded point after point, keeping his eyes on the one goal they all had in common: working together for independence.

Many, not understanding this logic, dubbed his move the Patna Surrender. But this "surrender" had a strange effect that was not lost on his secretary, Pyarelal: "The more he effaced himself, the more they needed him, and his weight and influence in their councils grew. His utter self-abnegation gave him power which no official position in the Congress or outside could have given."[21]

We might contrast this with an event from Poland in the 1980s, as the Solidarity struggle gained ground. Solidarity leader Lech Walesa was in the very act of signing an important agreement with the government when a coworker rushed in and told him to add a new issue—amnesty for the strikers who had been arrested in previous protests. Walesa agreed to add such a provision to the deal, and the government promptly pulled out, thus extending the Polish people's struggle several hard years more.

Clearly, then, our ability to compromise will depend on formulating and adhering to specific goals. The following guidelines should be kept in mind in choosing such goals.

- The goal must add to the welfare of all parties, and it is always possible to identify such an outcome. Remember that dissuading an oppressor from his oppression is as much a matter of his welfare as our own.

- The goal should never be frivolous or merely serve individual self-interest.

- The demands should be concrete, actionable, and realistic; only rarely should they be symbolic.

- Tacking new demands onto our list of goals when our campaign has gained some traction, however tempting, changes our interaction with the opponent from a conversation to a power play. This principle is sometimes called "no fresh issue."

Building it Right: The Secret of Constructive Program

The ultimate goal of all satyagraha is not simply to tear down an oppressive system but also to replace that system with something more positive. Again, this is strategic as well as a matter of principle: nothing helps to disestablish an unwanted regime more than building a wanted one. There is nothing as potent as community self-uplift in overcoming dependence and oppression.

This aspect of nonviolence is generally called a constructive program. In the long term, a constructive program provides the glue that keeps movements together, building on the spontaneous energy that may erupt in the face of some severe injustice and preventing that energy from melting away when the injustice has been addressed or the movement meets with unexpected resistance. These are strategic advantages that rest on the fact that nonviolence, as a positive force, lends itself even more natively to "cooperating with good," as King would say, than to "noncooperating with evil," though that, too, has its place.

Other strategic advantages follow from this principle. For instance, working together for an overriding goal makes for an effective and enduring bond among people.[22] Constructive work also can reassure the public, which may be frightened by even nonviolent resistance to an established authority, and it can undermine a repressive regime without provoking the reaction that confrontation does. Most importantly, a well-developed constructive program builds the infrastructure for a new society *before* the old society crumbles, preventing the emergence of a power vacuum into which new repressive elements often rush.

Even in insurrectionary struggles, therefore, constructive programs should have pride of place. Historians and activists alike have often neglected this undramatic but natural and very effective dimension of nonviolence (though among some activists, at least, this is beginning to change).

It was Gandhi who gave the principle its name, and his long struggle in South Africa and India, the most sustained nonviolent struggle yet known, is a model in this regard as in so many others. Gandhi drew on the inherently positive nature of nonviolence by emphasizing constructive work within the community as a complement to, and eventually the leading edge of, confrontation. Although we tend to think of dramatic showdowns such as the Salt Satyagraha or the Quit India movement as the story of satyagraha in India, Gandhi once explained to a friend that "My real politics is constructive work."[23]

Confrontational nonviolence, or what I like to call "obstructive program," can be very effective, indeed dramatically so, but it requires that we maintain momentum and group solidarity until an opportune moment arrives. It also requires that we make progress without provoking undue hostility from our opponents and that we demonstrate our underlying commitment to the well-being of all, so as to leave the least possible legacy of bitterness, neither of which is always easy. Finally, oppression operates on the false assumption that the oppressed are helpless and dependent, but confrontational nonviolence does not always help to convince ourselves, our people, and in time the oppressor that we can govern and provide for ourselves.

Very often, the remedy for such difficulties is found in proactive, sustained, concrete projects. For example, Israeli policy since 1948 has deliberately prevented the emergence of indigenous development initiatives by the Palestinians in order to foster their dependence on Israel.[24] This is why the "illegal" schools, barter markets, and many other things people did for each other during the first Palestinian Intifada, which demonstrated the falsity of this assumption, were a vital support for the insurrection. Likewise, one of the first campaigns Dolci carried out with Sicilian peasants was a constructive program called "strike in reverse." Unpaid villagers began building for themselves a road, which the state bureaucracy not only had postponed but also actually opposed. Police soon came to stop the work and put Dolci and others behind bars. In time, however, the road was constructed and the people discovered how they could take their community development into their own hands.

The Sicilian example demonstrates another aspect of constructive programs: it is often the very success of such programs that attracts repression. The opponent may understand the revolutionary power of such community initiatives and do anything possible to undermine them. He may have less *excuse* to attack these programs and their participants but may perceive more *need*. We should not be surprised or even displeased, therefore, when our constructive programs face such attacks. It is the nature of satyagraha, whether constructive or obstructive, to elicit a response in order to expose the violence lying concealed in an unjust system. Regrettable as they are, such attacks can make it clear to onlookers—and even to the oppressors themselves—that what the oppressors are doing is not right.

Ideally, a nonviolent campaign would start with individual empowerment, looking next for constructive options within the community, and ultimately confront obstructive forces, if necessary, from a position of strength. These same principles can be applied by individuals in innumerable situations.

Interestingly, the Occupy movements in the United States, which *began* as protests in September 2011, went on to take up some highly creative constructive actions after those protests had been broken up by the police. In late 2012, for instance, Occupy

Sandy and Occupy Oklahoma offered immense support to hurricane victims—more effective support, we might add, than agencies such as the Red Cross and the Federal Emergency Management Agency. The Occupy movement also has created a money cooperative as well as Strike Debt and Rolling Jubilee, which buy up people's debts and cancel them. In other words, the Occupy movement backed into constructive programs when their obstructive program was thwarted, and it came kind of naturally for them because, in addition to protests, they had already created constructive elements, such as food kitchens and highly democratic decision making.

In less acute situations today, countless widespread, apparently unrelated projects, ranging from community supported agriculture to the extremely important effort to reform the media, are quietly providing the backbone of nonviolent revolution—if and when we choose to incorporate them into a comprehensive strategy. There also is a growing movement toward restorative justice as a constructive response to our grossly dehumanizing and ineffective justice system.[25] More confrontational, but still within legal parameters, is the growing movement to overturn Citizens United, the Supreme Court doctrine that corporations have the same rights as human beings (and, by implication, that human beings have no more rights than abstract entities such as corporations). These projects in particular recommend themselves as particularly effective components of a constructive strategy.

Oppressive regimes can usually wait for a march or a demonstration to go away, but they cannot survive a cottage industry when they are trying to exploit a people or a free school when they are trying to indoctrinate the citizenry. Often, because of their violent orientation, oppressors do not even realize that constructive actions pose a threat until it's too late. The Viceroy of India, Lord Irwin, famously boasted that he was "not losing any sleep" over the Salt Satyagraha—and then Britain lost the whole Empire. In this case—and maybe only in this case—the world's general ignorance of nonviolence actually turned out to be an advantage!

In an ideal world, revolutionary changes could be accomplished through constructive programs alone; even the threat of satyagraha might not be necessary. Today's world is, however, far from ideal. It contains much exploitation and oppression, as well as structural and physical violence in many forms. In such a world, the ideal formula for liberation is to reduce as much inherent conflict as possible through constructive programs and to isolate and confront the rest through nonviolent struggle. *Be constructive wherever possible and obstructive when necessary*, always ensuring that your approach is informed by right intention and undertaken using right means.

five

Peering Into the Heart of Satyagraha

We have seen that nonviolence and satyagraha begin with ourselves, that we must prepare and train in order to approach any conflict with right intention. Likewise, satyagraha will only be successful if it employs right means, including proportional response, compromise, well-defined goals, and constructive programs, as appropriate. However, some aspects of satyagraha remain to be examined. For instance, how are we to react when our nonviolent approach seems not to be achieving any result, and equally importantly, how should we behave when we are successful? How many people does a movement require to achieve success, and how important are symbols to a movement?

Finally, many of us may wonder whether it is possible to misuse nonviolence or whether satyagraha always necessitates suffering on the part of those who employ it. An examination of these questions helps us to further define the heart of satyagraha.

Seeing the Real Results

A nonviolent act will always have a useful effect, will always do good work in people's minds and hearts. In this respect it's the exact opposite of violence, which always leaves a legacy of harm, bitterness, and alienation. Where nonviolence is similar to violence, however, is that it may or may not be effective in achieving just result we want.

When we think we see satyagraha or nonviolence failing, more often than not it's because the degree or depth of the nonviolence being offered doesn't match the intensity of the violence. A spontaneous protest with no training behind it and no strategy ahead of it is only the tip of the nonviolence iceberg; merely refraining from physical aggression is only an enabling condition for the full power of nonviolence. When a preliminary effort fails, therefore, we should not jump to the conclusion that nonviolence doesn't work. As a Turkish activist recently admitted, "We failed the method; it didn't fail us."

Another reason we sometimes think nonviolence has failed is that we don't notice how it operates under the surface, often leading to more significant results down the road than we may even have intended. As historian B. R. Nanda put it, "The fact is that satyagraha was not designed to seize any particular objective or to crush the opponent, but *to set in motion forces which would ultimately lead to a new equation*; in such a strategy it [is] perfectly possible to lose all the battles and still win the war" (italics added).[26]

A dramatic example of this occurred during the famous Salt Satyagraha to break the government monopoly on salt, which imposed severe hardship on poor Indians and had come to epitomize British colonial power in India. On May 21, 1930, about two thousand people went to the Dharsana Salt Works to "illegally" take back the salt that had come from their own seashores. Wave after wave of disciplined, unarmed volunteers, twenty-five at a time, walked toward the entrance of the plant and were beaten to the ground, mostly without so much as lifting an arm to protect themselves. At the end of that day, 320 volunteers were hospitalized, and two soon died from the savage beating.

The sacrifice of the Indian volunteers did not "work" in terms of its short-term goal: the salt works was not liberated and the tax was not repealed.[27] That is, the *battle* was lost. But when years of nonviolent preparation were put to the test and the people's discipline held, the "war" was won. Because the colonial power resorted to bamboo and iron while the protesters resisted with courage and endurance, with refusal to hate, the regime lost its legitimacy. The real nature of the regime was exposed and India was positioned to gain her freedom. It was only a matter of time.

In fact, when independence came, seventeen years later, India and Britain were able to terminate the exploitative relationship cordially. Unlike most exits from colonial situations, the two nations parted as friends. As the British historian Arnold Toynbee noted, Gandhi made it impossible for the British to go on ruling India, but he made it possible for them to leave without rancor and without humiliation.[28] This is a classic description of the effect of nonviolent action, but none of this was apparent on that May day at the Dharsana Salt Works.

This is not the only time in the history of nonviolence that apparent failures have turned out to contain the seeds of greater success. Because of the gap in time between the nonviolent action and its effects, however, we can easily miss the connection, and this is one reason that many people fail to grasp the power of nonviolence itself. In nonviolence, remember, we are looking for more than just an immediate, outward result. It may be quite important in the immediate sense to stop an impending war, to block a malicious "free trade" agreement, or to remove a dictator from power, and failing to accomplish that immediately can be a disappointment. However, because nonviolent conflict is not just a win/lose fight and because we are more interested in long-term results, we should not lose hope after a setback. In practicing nonviolence, we must learn to trust that long-term results—such as a less oppressive regime, reconciliation among all the parties, justice all around—are bound to follow. Admittedly, this kind of faith doesn't come easily. When sixty peaceful demonstrators were shot dead at Sharpeville, South Africa, in 1960, the African National Congress leaders decided that nonviolence was not enough to overcome the apartheid regime. They subsequently lost nearly thirty years trying to fight the regime with acts of violence before Nelson Mandela was released from prison and they regained their nonviolent momentum. Likewise, it is very hard not to lose heart after brutal repression of the type that took place at Tiananmen Square, but knowing the deeper logic of nonviolence can often help. It also may help to keep in mind historian Theodore Roszak's words: "People try nonviolence for a week, and when it doesn't 'work' they go back to violence, which hasn't worked for centuries."[29]

Coping with Success

Knowing that nonviolence is often a long-term project can help us avoid depression and demoralization when nonviolence seems (temporarily) to have failed. However, it is equally important to avoid elation when nonviolence *hasn't* failed, partly because, as we see, to quantify success or failure in nonviolence is a subtle task. For a nonviolent person, it's a success simply to stay nonviolent, even under great provocation.

But nonviolent campaigns certainly can and do succeed outwardly as well. In fact, recent studies have shown that nonviolent insurrections work twice as well as violent ones, and in one-third the time.[30] Indeed, as history gradually corrects its unconscious bias toward violence, more and more stories of successful collective resistance are coming to light.

For instance, under Vichy jurisdiction in southern France, Protestant minister André Trocmé and his wife, Magda, organized the entire community of Le Chambon-sur-Lignon to rescue Jewish and other refugees throughout the Occupation, ultimately saving thousands of people. The resisters' courage so impressed the Occupation's commanding officer that he refused, at great danger to himself, to allow the local Gestapo detachment to raid the rescue centers.

Meanwhile, a highly dramatic—and highly instructive—event was unfolding right in Berlin. On the first weekend of March 1943, Jews "of Aryan kin"—mainly husbands of non-Jewish wives—were rounded up for deportation to concentration camps. Contrary to all expectations, the wives and mothers of these men, eventually numbering nearly six thousand women, gathered in front of the Rosenstrasse detention center, demanding the return of their loved ones and refusing to leave. Within a few days, the Gestapo relented and released the men, some of whom had to be hastily recalled from concentration camps where they had already been sent. Virtually all of these men survived the war. Even more amazingly, because Gestapo officials in other European capitals had similar "mixed-race" populations on their hands and were looking to Berlin for guidance, this one brief demonstration has been credited with saving tens of thousands of lives.[31]

In other words, even one of the weakest forms of nonviolence—a spontaneous and brief demonstration by untrained people with little or no idea of how nonviolence works and no plan to follow up their immediate action—worked effectively against one of the most oppressive regimes in modern history. With some training and strategy, the results might have been even more impressive. These two examples, particularly the latter, refute an extremely common objection to arguments for nonviolence, that it never would have worked against the Nazis. Actually, it worked spectacularly—when it was tried.

When such successes come, there are things we can do to keep the nonviolent character of the interaction moving and ensure that our efforts don't go to waste. We have already noted the importance of not piling on a fresh issue, which transforms the conversation into a power struggle. Even more important, however, is to avoid triumphalism, like a football player spiking the ball after a touchdown.

During the intense negotiations in Montgomery, Alabama, that followed the yearlong bus boycott, an attorney for the city's bus company was concerned that giving into the protesters' demands would open the door for them to "go about boasting of a victory that they had won over the white people, and this we will not stand for." Reflecting on this, King reminded his coworkers that "through nonviolence we avoid the temptation of taking on the psychology of victors." This psychology belongs to the ages-old dynamic of me-against-you that sees life as a clash of separate parties, often over symbols. Nonviolent psychology, by contrast, avoids turning successes into "victories" that polarize and alienate opponents. Recall Toynbee's observation that Gandhi made it impossible for the British to go on ruling India but (or rather, partly *because*) he made it possible for them to leave without rancor and without humiliation.

The final idea to keep in mind when dealing with the success of a nonviolent action is that sometimes success should be regarded as merely a beginning. Chances are you're not done yet. In the intoxication of success, or simply out of exhaustion, many movements dissolve before the real problem is solved—which is ultimately to destroy the very *idea* of oppression, not just its embodiment in a particular group or person. The recent annals of nonviolence are full of disappointing setbacks that followed successful overthrows: think of the Philippines, Serbia, Egypt, Yemen, and the Ukraine, to name a few. Similarly, although the First Intifada in Palestine (1987–1993) came to a conclusion with the signing of the Oslo Accords, that accord fell far short of meaningful freedom for Palestine.

It almost seems that, in this business, nothing fails like success! But before we jump to that conclusion, remember that these movements were often, and understandably, not complete. As we have seen, a robust constructive element, complete with alternative institutions ready to move into the vacuum, often can prevent this. More often than not, dogged persistence, what Latin American activists call *firmesa permanente*, needs to be continued even beyond victory.

If we adhere to rules such as "no fresh issue" and avoid the psychology of victors, we position ourselves to enjoy a success that only nonviolence can give and no one can take away.

The Importance (or Not) of Numbers

Because nonviolence is, after all, soul force, built primarily on the "person power" within an individual, the individual person plays a more central role in nonviolence than in other kinds of conflict-related action—especially military action, which actually tries to negate the role of the individual through uniforms, indoctrination, a strict chain of command, and so forth. There are times, of course, when numbers help. A Ferdinand Marcos or a Hosni Mubarak can brush off a few hundred people gathered in the square below, but he can't ignore a couple of million—especially if they're still there after he has unleashed his firepower against them.

During the successful Philippines insurrection, the term "people power" was coined to express the collective power of the aroused populace. But one participant, Cardinal Jaime Sin, made this insightful observation: "It was amazing. It was *two million independent decisions.* Each one said, in his heart, 'I will do this,' and they went out" (italics added).[32] In other words, even people power is made up of what I call person power, the committed will of courageous individuals.

In nonviolence—which, wherever possible, relies on persuasion rather than on coercion—clarity of message can replace numbers. Even that great American, Henry David Thoreau, saw this. In speaking of slavery, he said, "I know this well, that if one thousand, if one hundred, if ten men whom I could name—if ten *honest* men only—ay, if *one* HONEST man . . . ceasing to hold slaves, were to actually withdraw from this co-partnership, and be locked up in the city jail therefore, it would be the abolition of slavery in America. For it matters not how small the beginning may seem to be: what is once well done is done forever."[33]

The fact is that such an individual with vision and determination will often gather numbers when they're needed. This is part of a principle that Gandhi called the law of progression, and he illustrates it with a colorful image: "The Ganga [Ganges] does not leave its course in search of tributaries. Even so does the satyagrahi not leave his path, which is sharp as the sword's edge. But as the tributaries spontaneously join the Ganga as it advances, so it is with the river that is satyagraha."[34]

So, numbers are important in satyagraha—except when they're not. And when they are important, the right person can often gather them. This is worth bearing in mind, because when we are not quite aware of our own strength (which is often), we naturally reach out for the strength in numbers. This is natural, but it should not distract us from exploring the power within.

While the British were preoccupied by World War II, Gandhi felt he could not suspend the freedom struggle, but at the same time he was reluctant to breach his principle of non-embarrassment, which we mentioned in relation to his struggle in the 1913 South African railroad strike. The solution? He appointed one person, his trusted follower Vinoba Bhave, who was widely regarded as his spiritual successor, to perform civil disobedience and to court arrest. Thus, the British got the point that satyagraha was not going away, but they had to appreciate the courtesy of its temporary suspension while they were preoccupied and could not give their full attention to the "conversation" about freedom. Note that this tactic was not an empty symbol: Vinoba was a real person, noncooperating with real laws and paying a real penalty to signal to the regime that the struggle for freedom was not going away. Nonetheless, he was only one person.

Numbers are essential at times, but clarity of purpose and commitment are essential always. If a movement stays on course, people will join it when they're needed.

How Useful Are Symbols?

Symbols, like numbers, are of limited use in satya-graha—recall that *satyagraha* means "clinging to truth." And, as with our overestimation of the importance of numbers, we have tended to overuse symbols. Perhaps the most tragic example of a symbol gone wrong is the June 4, 1989, massacre in Beijing's Tiananmen Square. Students, workers, and many supporters gathered in vast numbers to demonstrate their solidarity and desire for reform. Because they lacked a long-term strategy, however, the square itself and their refusal to leave it became a symbol of their disobedience and a distrac-tion from the eminently legitimate goal of democratic reforms. We all know the results. On the other hand, if the resisters had left the square and gone back to their universities and villages to educate the people and to take concrete, achievable steps for change, the democ-racy movement in China—and the brave people who embodied it—might still be alive.

This does not mean that sit-ins and occupations are never effective. When tens of thousands of indige-nous protesters nonviolently took over the Ecuadorean Congress in 2000, it had a telling effect, although the movement leaders were outmaneuvered and lost power within a matter of days. Two years later, however, af-ter extensive low-profile grassroots organizing, one of these leaders was elected president.

The Ecuador uprising was similar to the upris-ing in Tiananmen Square, but there were three differences that probably contributed to its eventual success. First, the protesters did not occupy a mere symbol of power, but a *place* of power. Second, they acted when they were strong enough to take power, not merely to ask for it. And third, they were able to carry on after the occupation ended—that is, the occupation had a past and a future and was part of a larger campaign that could deploy a variety of tactics, confrontational and other.

Tenacity certainly can make the difference between success and failure in nonviolence, as in anything else. That persistence, though, should be reserved for the real and only rarely for symbols of something real. In the famous Salt March of 1930, Gandhi showed master showmanship and control of symbolic expression, walking more than two hundred miles to the sea to break the unjust salt laws by the simplest possible act of picking up a pinch of salt. But it is often forgotten that he was going to the real sea to collect real salt—an act that was constructive and concrete—and, in this case, illegal. Similarly, his Great March in South Africa fifteen years earlier was not just a protest; he had to move three thousand striking miners and their now-homeless families to his ashram, or spiritual community. Again, the action was technically against the law. Neither of these marches, in other words, was *merely* symbolic; they were very concrete actions that had also some symbolic resonance. Thus, although symbols can enhance or grow out of concrete actions, they should never take the place of concrete actions.

Can Nonviolence Be Misused?

Nonviolence, when practiced correctly, cannot be misused. Unfortunately, however, the fair *name* of nonviolence can be abused—and it frequently is. When a gun-owners group in California referred to their refusal to register their assault rifles as "civil disobedience," for instance, they were forgetting that owning a deadly weapon is the farthest extreme from civility or nonviolence.

It is also possible for nonviolent *tactics*—or rather, tactics that also find a place in nonviolence—to be used in a not-nonviolent context. In 1991, marchers sought to enter Gujarat state in India to protest against the construction of dams on the Narmada River, a process that had already flooded hundreds of villages and had many environmentally and socially destructive consequences. But, Gujarati government officials, who had their own misguided reasons for wanting the dam, mustered out schoolchildren to block the march while singing Gandhian songs!

This is why it's so important to keep people who still espouse violence from muddying the waters of a nonviolent movement. In today's demonstrations or other nonviolent actions, this is as important as being able to stand firm on essential goals but compromise on anything else. During the fundamentally nonviolent Occupy movement, for example, there were those who felt it was OK to use "a little" violence—to break a window here or burn a trash bin there—in the name of what they called "diversity of tactics." But this is a corruption of nonviolence. Even when one takes the question out of the moral arena and looks at the question of *effectiveness*, especially long-term effectiveness, it's clear that even "a little" violence renders a nonviolence movement ambiguous and therefore weak. In other words, the difference between violence and nonviolence is not one of "diversity," like the difference between robins and sparrows. Rather, they are opposites and have opposite effects. And nonviolence is not a tactic, anyway, but a living power.

The Role of Suffering in Satyagraha

In Auschwitz concentration camp in 1942, ten Polish prisoners were being taken off to die of starvation in an underground cell because one prisoner had escaped. To everyone's surprise, another prisoner stepped forward and asked to die in the place of one of those unfortunate men. This was Father Maximilian Kolbe, now known as the Saint of Auschwitz. Although he was in fact put to death some days later, his inspiring sacrifice made a huge difference to the morale of the prisoners, probably saving hundreds who would otherwise have succumbed to despair and thus—in those unbearable conditions—to death.

By the time a conflict requires satyagraha (that is, by the time it reaches Stage 2 of our figure in Chapter 3) some people must already be suffering, but their suffering, unwillingly endured, is not awakening the hearts of their opponents. In fact, if it is left unaddressed, an unjust situation can eventually begin to seem normal, just an example of how life is, or even the victim's own fault. Consider the protracted sufferings of the Palestinians in the Occupied Territories, the ethnic Albanians in Kosovo in the 1990s, or those millions living in desperate poverty today. These are among the countless unfortunate victims of structural violence— suffering imposed by unjust social or political structures rather than by outward force and violence, though it is often backed up by direct force or violence as well.

Whenever it happens that we can no longer accept such oppression, we have the option of making ourselves a lightning rod for the suffering it is imposing in order to awaken others and end it. Father Kolbe's action is an example of this. Likewise, the students involved with the ill-fated White Rose conspiracy mounted against the Nazi regime in Munich at the height of World War II hoped the risk they were running would have a similar effect when they issued pamphlets calling for passive resistance, though they hardly knew what such resistance would look like and could not have realized that passive resistance is only one aspect of true nonviolence or satyagraha. They knew they were facing almost certain death—and ultimately only one of them escaped this fate—but they reasoned, "Better an end in terror than a terror without end." That is the moral calculus we may have to make in cases of extreme oppression.

Fasting in Satyagraha

Death is less likely in nonviolence than it is in violent conflicts, but as Father Kolbe and the White Rose conspirators showed, sometimes it is necessary to put our lives on the line. Fasting, especially an open-ended fast or a "fast unto death," as Gandhi called it, is one form this drastic remedy can take. To fast as part of a Stage 3 act of persuasion in a nonviolent struggle, especially if it could end in one's own death, *can* be a powerful way to awaken others to the wrongness of a situation and your willingness to take on any suffering to correct it. However, this method can coerce rather than persuade, making it contrary to the spirit of satyagraha. Therefore, fasting as an act of satyagraha (as opposed to an act of personal purification) should be undertaken only as the very last resort, and even then only under very specific conditions.

- First, *the faster must be certain that he or she is the right person to make such a sacrifice.* This requires control of one's desires, even the desire to live, and should not be motivated by hatred of the opponent.

- Second, *the action should be directed toward people who can conceivably be reached by the extreme act.* If they don't have even that degree of concern, or don't understand the logic of sacrifice (as is often the case in the West), fasting is the wrong technique.

- Third, *the fast should be designed to bring about some realistic goal.* A general desire for "world peace" or the like, though noble, is not achievable by fasting, as is nearly always the case, the fasters have not previously gained a powerful grip on the imagination of millions of people.

• *Fourth, fasting should only be undertaken in the context of a truly nonviolent campaign.* The fast of the Irish Republican Army prisoners in Long Kesh prison, for instance, did not meet any of these criteria; thus, despite the courage and sacrifice of the fasters, ten people lost their lives without resulting in any visible social change.

• *Finally, remember that fasting shouldn't be offered until and unless all other options have been exhausted.*

When these requirements are met, fasting can work wonders. Gandhi was a famous master of this technique. His "epic fast" in 1932 caused the British to withdraw separate electorates for caste and noncaste Hindus, and his "miracle of Calcutta" fast of 1946 ended communal rioting that the police and army had been unable to control. Even so, Gandhi came to feel that, in the end, a few of his fasts had been coercive and therefore, from his point of view, failures.

Taking Control

In satyagraha, we do not seek suffering for its own sake, nor do we seek to make martyrs of ourselves. But we understand the profound difference between the passive suffering that millions undergo, with no noticeable effect, and the willingness to take suffering on oneself, as Father Kolbe did, for a higher cause—when there's no other way. It's the latter kind of suffering, what King called "unearned suffering," that engages the power of nonviolence.

Nonviolent struggles, especially in a late-stage conflict, can be rough. So it is good to remind ourselves that, in the long run, the suffering undertaken voluntarily in a nonviolent struggle will be far less than the suffering caused either by accepting an unjust situation or by using violence to overcome it. For instance, although a thousand or so people died during the Indian freedom struggle, particularly in the Amritsar Massacre of 1919, *millions* of people died as passive victims, such as during the "Bengal famine" of 1943, when almost the entire rice crop of the country was confiscated for the British army. Likewise, as King pointed out, more people were killed during six nights of rioting in Detroit than during six years of civil disobedience in the South.

There are two rules of thumb about suffering, when it has become unavoidable. First, the sooner we can respond to a conflict actively and nonviolently, the less we will have to suffer to resolve it. And second, the more we are prepared to suffer voluntarily, the less we will have to suffer involuntarily.

six

What Have We Learned?

Nonviolence is an innate capacity of human nature. It is not a moral commandment; still less is it a philosophical abstraction. Nonviolence, at least the kind I've presented here, is an energy that operates in and on all living beings. It can be understood, predicted, and controlled like many other forces in nature. Probably the most important thing we need to know about nonviolence is that it's not the *absence* of anything as much as it is a *positive force*. It is the force of love, though at times it may not feel that way. The U.S. Civil Rights movement, King explained, did not cause outbursts of anger but "expressed anger under discipline for maximum effect." This discipline of conserving our anger is not an act of repression. When we do it correctly, it enables our anger to be converted into a creative power. Nonviolence is the power released by the conversion of a negative drive.

That transformation of negative or disruptive energies within the human being is not only a growth process for the individual; it can have an astounding effect on opponents—an effect that threats and weapons cannot match. During the successful Philippines People Power Revolution of 1986—which is only one example among thousands we could cite—soldiers defied direct orders from their superiors and refused to fire on peaceful protesters. In many cases, they were actually seen to break down in tears and defect.[35]

Observing this effect, Kenneth Boulding, a founder of modern peace research, coined the term "integrative power," which he compared to "threat power" and "exchange power."[36] Integrative power is the power released when we make a commitment to bear witness to the truth of our interconnectedness, even when our opponent is doing violence to that truth, and perhaps to our persons. The opponent sees himself as radically separate from us, whereas we can see the unity he has lost sight of and can thereby help him to see it as well. The result, Boulding points out, is that both parties end up closer. When we control the divisive drives within us for this purpose, then "control" does not mean "repress." Gandhi was quite familiar with this dynamic: "I have learnt through bitter experience the one supreme lesson to conserve my anger, and as heat conserved is transmuted into energy, even so our anger controlled can be transmuted into a power that can move the world."[37]

King adds some clarification to that transmuting process in his above-quoted (and worth repeating) statement that the Civil Rights activists controlled anger and *released it under discipline* for maximum effect. Seen in this light, it becomes intriguingly clear that the power of nonviolence is latent within us, waiting to be released, if we check the tendency to act from a place of anger or fear. If we define nonviolence as the force released by the conversion of a negative drive, such as fear or anger that would tear people apart if expressed in its raw forms, the converse is that those negative forces and their expression are known as violence.

A Way of Being

So nonviolence is not a moral or philosophical abstraction. It also is not just a set of tactics, a mere method. People fighting for their freedom have brought about impressive changes simply by not taking up weapons. As a Yemeni protester said to a friend of mine in 2012, "They can't defeat us because we've left our guns at home!" But deeper and more lasting changes happen when we leave our *hatred* at home.

Once we have mastered this trick—and I hope this book has provided some insight into how to do this—we can see the violence in our world today in a more optimistic and more challenging light. All this anger, whether roused by the mass media, by the gross inequalities in our economy, or whatever, is raw material for nonviolence! To express it in its raw form would be a waste.

Many people think of nonviolence as a tactic to be adopted when they have no better choice, because any violence from them would meet with fierce repression, or because they just plain don't have the necessary weapons, and they often reserve the right to go back to violence if they do not meet with success. Whatever may be the merits of this approach—and it is any day better and can require more courage than violence—I hope I've made it clear that we can go much further when we hold nonviolence as a principle, a way of being in the world.

In this approach, nonviolence is not really the recourse of the weak but actually calls upon an uncommon kind of strength; it is not a refraining from something but the engaging of a positive force. The more we are able to act—and be—without hatred, the more we are able to resist what someone is *doing* without wishing them any harm, the more we are able to "liquidate antagonism but not the antagonists themselves," in Gandhi's words,[38] the more available this power or force becomes. In a way that we don't yet understand, this attitude and worldview of interconnectedness unlocks energies that lead to deeper and more permanent change.

To say that nonviolence is not merely a strategy does not mean that no strategy is necessary. As we have seen, this is far from true. But there's a remarkable fea-

ture of nonviolence that cannot be claimed by milita-
rism or violence: that carrying out the principle is *also*
effective strategy. Unlike violence, where we bank on
the hopeless idea that wrong means can bring about a
right end, in nonviolence we do not have to choose
between the right thing and the most effective thing to
do. In the long run, they're the same. If you pass up an
opportunity to humiliate someone, for example, simply
because you believe on principle that everyone is enti-
tled to respect, it gives you a nearly infallible strategy to
bring them closer. As Nobel Peace Prize winner Adolfo
Perez Esquivel put it, "Nonviolent action implants, by
anticipation within the very process of change itself,
the values to which it will ultimately lead. Hence it
does not sow peace by means of war. It does not attempt to build up by tearing down."[39]

A Movement Oversweeping
the World

In 1939, Gandhi wrote, "My optimism rests on my
belief in the infinite possibilities of the individual to
develop nonviolence. The more you develop it in your
own being, the more infectious it becomes till it over-
whelms your surroundings and by and by might over-
sweep the world."[40] In the years since Gandhi penned
those words, though they have been violent years, the
world has also begun to see just such an awakening.
In fact, it has been estimated that more than half the

world now lives in a society that has been significantly affected by a nonviolent movement.[41]

The modern history of nonviolence has been aided by several qualitative changes that are potentially of immense help in "oversweeping the world." First, we are learning that every culture has local ways of responding creatively to conflict, and that these approaches can be mobilized in the context of a protracted nonviolent struggle. For instance, indigenous people, who play a critical role in environmental struggles, are beginning to organize and network among themselves.

Second, we now know that nonviolence can be carried out without a single charismatic leader if there is no such person on hand, which is most of the time. However, movements can be aided materially by the intervention of peace teams or the help of a skilled outsider. Moreover—and this may be the most important development of all—people are learning as never before how to teach others what they've gained from the successes and failures of their own movements. For example, the Center for Advanced Nonviolent Actions and Strategies has sent veterans of the successful Otpor rebellion that overthrew President Slobodan Milosevic in 2000 to Egypt and other places facing similar struggles.

Third, the majority of the movements that have been nonviolent, in one way or another, in the years since Gandhi and King—and they are many—have been almost exclusively obstructive, like the cascade of insurrections called the "color revolutions" in Eastern

Europe and the Arab Spring that followed. A few have been almost exclusively *constructive*; the largest and most dramatic example of such a movement being the MST, or Landless Worker Movement, in Brazil, which has given land and livelihood to tens of thousands of families and created communities in the process—but has not found a creative way to deal with resistance from landowners. With few exceptions—such as the First Intifada in Palestine, which ran from 1987 to 1993—we have not seen a sustained campaign that, like the Indian freedom struggle, could operate in both modes and had a way to decide strategically when to be obstructive and when to be constructive.

Nonetheless, there is growing awareness of this possibility, and when *that* kind of movement happens once more, building on a progression from personal empowerment to constructive program, to satyagraha when needed (and it probably will be), we may well start to see the full power of nonviolence to change our world.[42]

Finally, modern science has dramatically shifted from an emphasis on rational materialism (and the separateness and meaninglessness that such a view entails) to a more robust picture of human nature and the world that is surprisingly consistent with timeless wisdom traditions. This picture of innate empathy and cooperation, confirmed by both wisdom and science, paves the way for a cultural story in which nonviolence would be as much at home as violence is at home—however we may consider it an unwelcome guest—today.

"Those who are attracted to nonviolence," Gandhi wrote, "should join the experiment," and it has become clearer with each passing year that nothing less than the survival of life on earth could be at stake. I hope that the glimpse into the history and potential of nonviolence that I've offered here, brief as it is, serves to show that although it will call for work and sacrifice, we can use this power to redirect human destiny to a higher goal. This is the most compelling challenge of our time.

Highlights:
A Handy Reference

"Nonviolence is the law of our species." [page 2]

"What satyagraha does . . . is not to suppress reason but to free it from inertia and to establish its sovereignty over prejudice, hatred, and other baser passions. In other words, if one may paradoxically put it, it does not enslave, it compels reason to be free." [page 11]

It is not me against you but you and me against the problem. [page 14]

Try never to humiliate or to accept humiliation, for that hurts everyone. [pages 14–15]

The more you respect the humanity of your opponent, the more effectively you can oppose his or her injustice. [page 15]

"Real noncooperation is noncooperation with evil, and not with the evildoer." [page 16]

Because all violence begins in the failure or refusal to recognize another as fully human, the deeper reaches of nonviolence must involve (re)awakening the humanity of one's opponent. [page 17]

Meditation is a great humanizer. [page 19]

Nonviolence is the power released by the conversion of a negative drive. [page 63]

"I have learnt through bitter experience the one supreme lesson to conserve my anger, and as heat conserved is transmuted into energy, even so our anger controlled can be transmuted into a power that can move the world." [page 65]

Let us not forget that our own personal freedom from anger, fear, and so forth is no small benefit of the practice of nonviolence. [page 17]

"Things of fundamental importance to the people are not secured by reason alone but have to be purchased with their suffering. . . . If you want something really important to be done you must not merely satisfy the reason, you must move the heart also." [page 23]

Be constructive wherever possible and obstructive when necessary. [page 38]

Gandhi made it impossible for the British to go on ruling India, but he made it possible for them to leave without rancor and without humiliation. [page 45]

"People try nonviolence for a week, and when it doesn't 'work' they go back to violence, which hasn't worked for centuries." [page 45]

Numbers are essential at times, but clarity of purpose and commitment are essential always. [page 51]

Although symbols can enhance or grow out of concrete actions, they should never take the place of concrete actions. [page 53]

The sooner we can respond to a conflict actively and nonviolently, the less we will have to suffer to resolve it. [page 59]

The more we are prepared to suffer voluntarily, the less we will have to suffer involuntarily. [page 59]

In nonviolence we do not have to choose between the right thing and the most effective thing to do. [page 66]

Notes

1. Harijan, September 1936. Gandhi was essentially translating a common phrase found in the Indian epics and other literature: *ahimsa, paramo dharma*, "Nonviolence is the supreme law," the fundamental upholding principle of the universe.

2. Christian Peacemaker Teams, *Year in Review February 2010–31 (October 2010)*.

3. It is difficult to find an overview of the "new science," which involves so many disciplines and is filling in rapidly. For a starting point, see the Metta Center Web site, mettacenter.org.

4. Andrew Young, *A Way Out of No Way* (Nashville: Thomas Nelson, 1996).

5. Much of this evidence is assembled by Jeremy Rifkin in *The Empathic Civilization* (New York: Penguin/Tarcher, 2009).

6. Martin Luther King Jr., *Stride toward Freedom: The Montgomery Story* (New York: Harper & Brothers, 1958).

7. See, for example, Sharp's documentary film *Where There Is Hatred* (Maryknoll, NY: Maryknoll World Productions, 1990) or *Waging Nonviolent Struggle* (Boston: Porter Sargent Publishers, 2005).

8. Interested readers can find many tactics in Part 2 of Gene Sharp's classic work *The Politics of Nonviolent Action* (Boston: Porter Sargent Publishers, 1973), although from a principled point of view a few of his 198 tactics would not quite fit, such as those that involve shaming one's opponent. For the less drastic situations we all face in life, the techniques of nonviolent communication worked out in Marshall Rosenberg, *Nonviolent Communication: A Language of Life* (Encinitas, CA: Puddle-Dancer Press) are very useful.

9. M. K. Gandhi, *Hind Swaraj or Indian Home Rule* (Ahmedabad, Gujarat: Navajivan, 1938), 70.

10. M. K. Gandhi, *Satyagraha in South Africa* (Ahmedabad: Navajivan, 1928), 433.

11. Staughton Lynd and Alice Lynd, *Nonviolence in America* (Maryknoll, NY: Orbis, 1995), 399.

12. Council for a Parliament of the World's Religions, *Declaration toward a Global Ethic* (Chicago: Council for a Parliament of the World's Religions, 1993), 5.

13. N. K. Bose, ed., *Selections from Gandhi* (Ahmedabad, Gujarat: Navajivan, 1948), 221.

14. *Hadith of Jabir*, 1497.

15. M. K. Gandhi, "Nonviolent Resistance," on the train to Wardha, April 5, 1942, in *Collected Works of Mahatma Gandhi* 82, no. 199.

16. Ralph Summy, "Nonviolence and the Case of the Extremely Ruthless Opponent," *Pacifica Review* 6, no. 1 (May 1994): 1–29.

17. These five practices are the basis of a complete campaign strategy based on nonviolent principles, offered as Metta's Roadmap, mettacenter.org/roadmap.

18. We recommend passage meditation as taught by Sri Eknath Easwaran. See easwaran.org or our e-book, *Meditation for Peacemakers*, at mettacenter.org/research-education/publications.

19. John Malkin, "In Engaged Buddhism, Peace Begins with You," *Shambala Sun* (July 2003).

20. M. K. Gandhi, *Young India*, May 11, 1931.

21. Pyarelal and Sushila Nayar, *In Gandhiji's Mirror* (Oxford: Oxford India Series, 2004), 213.

22. Consider, for example, the famous Robbers Cave experiment, detailed in Muzafer Sherif, *In Common Predicament* (Boston: Houghton Mifflin, 1966), and Muzafer Sherif et al., *The Robbers Cave Experiment* (Wesleyan, OH: Wesleyan University Press, 1961).

23. Pyarelal and Sushila Nayar, *In Gandhiji's Mirror*, 268.

24. Souad Dajani, "Nonviolent Resistance in the Occupied Territories: A Critical Reevaluation," in Stephen Zunes, Lester R. Kurtz, and Sarah Beth Asher (eds.), *Nonviolent Social Movements: A Geographical Perspective* (Malden, MA: Blackwell Publishers, 1999), 53–54.

25. The best clearinghouse for information about the growing movement for restorative justice is restorativejustice.org.

26. *India News*, October 1, 1994, 11.

27. For a full discussion of what I call "work" versus work, see Chapter 4 of Michael N. Nagler, *The Search for a Nonviolent Future*, 2nd ed. (Novato, CA: New World Library, 2004).

28. Arnold Toynbee, 1960, "India's Contribution to World Unity," Azad Memorial Lectures.

29. Quoted in Petra K. Kelly, *Thinking Green! Essays on Environmentalism, Feminism, and Nonviolence* (Berkeley, CA: University of California, 1994).

30. Erica Chenoweth and Maria J. Stephan, *Why Civil Resistance Works: The Strategic Logic of Nonviolent Conflict* (New York: Columbia University Press, 2011).

31. Nathan Stoltzfus, *Resistance of the Heart* (New York: W.W. Norton, 1996). I do not recommend the film based on this story because it overlooks the effectiveness of nonviolence in favor of Hollywood-style sexuality.

32. Stephen Zunes, Lester R. Kurtz, and Sarah Beth Asher (eds.), *Nonviolent Social Movements*, 151.

33. Henry David Thoreau, "Resistance to Civil Government," in Jeffrey S. Cramer (ed.) *Henry D. Thoreau: Essays* (New Haven: Yale University, 2013), 156–157. This essay was later known as "On the Duty of Civil Disobedience." It is not known whether Thoreau actually ever used the latter term.

34. M. K. Gandhi, *Satyagraha in South Africa*, trans. V. G. Desai (Ahmedabad, Gujarat: Navajivan Publishing House, 1950).

35. Stephen Zunes, "The Origins of People Power in the Philippines," in Stephen Zunes, Lester R. Kurtz, and Sarah Beth Asher (eds.), *Nonviolent Social Movements*, 129–157.

36. Kenneth Boulding, *The Three Faces of Power* (Newbury Park, CA: Sage Publications, 1989).

37. M. K. Gandhi, *Young India*, September 15, 1920.

38. See note 13 on previous page.

39. Adolfo Perez Esquivel, *Christ in a Poncho: Testimonials of the Nonviolent Struggles in Latin America* (New York: Orbis Books, 1984), 127.

40. M. K. Gandhi, *Harijan*, January 28, 1939.

41. See Richard Deats, "The Global Spread of Active Nonviolence," in Walter Wink, ed., *Peace Is the Way* (Maryknoll, MA: Orbis Books, 2000). And much has happened since then!

42. The Metta Center created the Roadmap Project for exactly this purpose. Visit mettacenter.org/roadmap for more information.

Acknowledgments

I have the special enjoyment of writing on the eve of Thanksgiving 2013 some words of thanks to the many who have helped me in the creation of this book. In the first instance let me give thanks and deep reverence, as always, to my teacher, Sri Eknath Easwaran, without whom I would not have had either the understanding or the confidence to write anything about nonviolence and Gandhi, and to the love and support of my spiritual family who saw me through this process. Likewise, I want to thank everyone at Metta, especially Stephanie Van Hook, without whose tireless dedication and understanding Metta would hardly be what it is today, and Anna Leinberger, who smuggled a very rough copy of what was to become *The Nonviolence Handbook* into the office of Berrett-Koehler, leading to the most rewarding experience I have ever had with a publisher. Although BK is itself a kind of family, I would like to specially thank Jeevan Sivasubramaniam, the managing director, who long ago saw that I might have something to add to their goal of "building a world that works for all," and freelance editor extraordinaire Todd Manza, who brought the book out with such skill when the manuscript, complete with infelicities, landed on his desk. Any errors that remain are despite, not because of, their skillful work.

For Further Reading and Viewing

Books

Ackerman, Peter, and Jack DuVall. *A Force More Powerful: A Century of Nonviolent Conflicts*. New York: St. Martin's Press, 2000.

Bartkowski, Maciej. *Recovering Nonviolent History: Civil Resistance in Liberation Struggles*. Boulder, CO: Lynn Rienner, 2013.

Chenoweth, Erica, and Stephan, Maria J. *Why Civil Resistance Works: The Strategic Logic of Nonviolent Conflict*. New York: Columbia University Press, 2011.

Easwaran, Eknath. *Gandhi the Man*. Petaluma, CA: Nilgiri Press, 1997.

_____. *Nonviolent Soldier of Islam: A Man to Match his Mountains—Badshah Khan*. Petaluma, CA: Nilgiri Press, 1984.

Gandhi, M. K. *All Men are Brothers*. Ahmedabad, Gujarat: Navajivan, 1960.

_____. *An Autobiography: The Story of My Experiments with Truth*. Translated by Mahadev Desai. Boston: Beacon Press, 1927.

_____. *Hind Swaraj or Indian Home Rule*. Ahmedabad, Gujarat: Navajivan, 1938.

_____. *Satyagraha in South Africa*. Translated by V. G. Desai. Ahmedabad, Gujarat: Navajivan, 1950.

_____. *Vows and Observances*. Berkeley, CA: Berkeley Hills, 1999.

Gandhi, Rajmohan. *Gandhi, His People, and the Empire*. Berkeley: University of California, 2008. (Probably the best all-round biography.)

King, Martin Luther, Jr. *A Testament of Hope: The Essential Writings and Speeches of Martin Luther King, Jr.* Edited by James Melvin Washington. San Francisco: Harper San Francisco, 1991.

Lynd, Staughton, and Alice Lynd. *Nonviolence in America: A Documentary History*. Maryknoll, NY: Orbis, 1995.

Mahoney, L., and L. Eguren. *Unarmed Bodyguards: International Accompaniment for the Protection of Human Rights*. West Hartford, CT: Kumarian, 1997.

McManus, Philip, and Gerald Schlabach (eds.). *Relentless Persistence: Nonviolent Action in Latin America*. Eugene, OR: Wipf and Stock Publishers, 2004.

Nagler, Michael. *The Search for a Nonviolent Future*. 2nd ed. Novato, CA: New World Library, 2004.

Prabhu, R. K., and U. R. Rao. *The Mind of Mahatma Gandhi*. Ahmedabad, Gujarat: Navajivan, 1960. (I consider this well-indexed collection the most useful all-round.)

Roberts, Adam, and Timothy Garton Ash. *Civil Resistance and Power Politics: The Experience of Non-violent Action from Gandhi to the Present*. Oxford: Oxford University, 2009.

Sharp, Gene. *The Politics of Nonviolent Action*. Boston: Porter Sargent, 1973.

Stoltzfus, Nathan. *Resistance of the Heart: Intermarriage and the Rosenstrasse Protest in Nazi Germany*. New York: Norton, 1996.

Wink, Walter (ed.). *Peace Is the Way: Writings on Nonviolence from the Fellowship of Reconciliation*. New York: Orbis, 2000.

Zunes, Stephen, Lester R. Kurtz, and Sarah Beth Asher (eds.). *Nonviolent Social Movements: A Geographical Perspective*. Malden, MA: Blackwell Publishers, 1999.

Training and Organizing Manuals

Galtung, Johan. *Conflict Transformation by Peaceful Means: The Transcend Method*. New York: United Nations, 2000.

Hunter, Daniel. *Direct Action Training Manual*. 2010. E-book available at trainingforchange.org/node/637. (Many other resources, including their Third-Party Nonviolent Intervention Curriculum, are available at trainingforchange.org.)

Moyer, Bill. *The Movement Action Plan: A Strategic Framework Describing the Eight Stages of Successful Social Movements*. 1987. Available online at historyisaweapon.com/defcon1/moyer-map.html.

Moyer, Bill, JoAnn McAllister, Mary Lou Finley, and Steven Soifer. *Doing Democracy: The MAP Model for Organizing Social Movements*. Gabriola Island, British Columbia: New Society Publishers, 2001.

Tactics

In addition to Gene Sharp's classic list, see now Andrew Boyd and Richard Miller's *Beautiful Trouble: A Toolbox for Revolution*. New York and London: OR Books, 2012. As with Sharp, most but not all of these can be carried out with nonviolent intention.

Some Videos

Documentary histories of recent nonviolent insurrections.

A Force More Powerful. York Zimmerman, 2000. Three-part survey of several key resistance and insurrectionary movements. Film and book available from the International Center for Nonviolent Conflict.

Bringing Down a Dictator. York Zimmerman, 2001–2002. On the overthrow of President Milosevic by the 2000 Otpor student uprising in Serbia.

Pray the Devil Back to Hell. Passion River Films, 2009. Inspiring story of the successful women's uprising in Liberia, which led to Nobel Prizes for Leemah Gbowee and others.

And finally: [although this is not, of course, a documentary] *Gandhi.* Columbia Pictures, 1982. Moving and for the most part highly accurate. See my audio talk for commentary, mettacenter.org/research-education/audio-resources-mp3/.

On the Web

In addition to private ventures such as gandhiserve.org and gandhifoundation.net, the government of India has recently put online a nearly complete resource for the vast collection of writings by and about Gandhi, at gandhiheritageportal.org.

The most comprehensive resource on nonviolent campaigns, past and present, is the Global Nonviolent Action Database, nvdatabase.swarthmore.edu, housed at Swarthmore College under the direction of Professor George Lakey.

Regular writing and blogs on nonviolence are available at wagingnonviolence.org, popularresistance.org, fnvw.org (Friends for a Nonviolent World), gandhiking.ning.com (the Martin Luther King, Jr. Research and Education Institute, Stanford), and of course, mettacenter.org.

Index

freedom struggle in, as
sustained campaign, 64
independence for, 1, 42, 46,
67
protest against dam construction on Narmada
River, 52
Quit India movement, 34
Salt Satyagraha in, 34, 38,
41–42, 51
willingness to risk dying in
freedom struggle in, 24
infrastructure for new society,
33–38
inner strength. *See* courage;
empowerment; "person
power"
"integrative power," 59
interconnectedness, 13–14, 61.
See also dignity of the
person
Iraq War, 2, 28–29
Irish Republican Army, 56
Irwin, Lord, 38
Israel, 35
Italy, 30

Japan, vi, vii, 16
Jeju Island, South Korea, vii
Jews, 44–45, 53
justice system, 37

Khan, Khan Abdul Ghaffar, 13
King, Martin Luther, Jr.
Christmas Sermon on Peace
(1967) by, 28
and civil rights movement
generally, 1
on "cooperating with good,"
33
on Detroit riots, 57
faith tradition of, 13
on "passive resistance," 5–6
on "psychology of victors," 46
on suffering, 28, 57
on transformation of anger,
58–59, 60

on unity of human family,
13–14
Kolbe, Father Maximilian, 53,
54, 55, 57
Kosovo, 54

labeling, 17–18, 22
Landless Worker Movement
(MST), 64
Latin America, 47. *See also*
specific countries
law of progression, 48
law of suffering, 23–24. *See also*
suffering
Le Chambon-sur-Lignon,
France, 44
Lincoln, Abraham, 18
love, 58

Mandela, Nelson, 43
Marcos, Ferdinand, 47
mass media, 18–19, 25, 37, 60
me-against-you attitude, 46, 66
media, 18–19, 25, 37, 60
mediation, 22–23
meditation, 19, 66, 69n18
Metta Center for Nonviolence,
69n17, 70n42, 82–83
military action. *See also* violence;
and specific countries
deaths from, 24, 26
impact of violence on
soldiers, 2
labeling of enemy by soldiers,
18
limited resources for, 15
negation of role of individual
in, 47
ultimate sacrifice in, 26
Milosevic, Slobodan, 63
mirror neurons, 5
misuse of nonviolence, 52–53
Montgomery, Ala., 45–46
MST (Landless Worker
Movement), 64
Mubarak, Hosni, 47
Muhammad, Prophet, 15

About the Author

Michael Nagler is one of the most respected scholars and advocates of nonviolence worldwide. He is Professor Emeritus of Classics and Comparative Literature at the University of California, Berkeley, where he founded the Peace and Conflict Studies Program, now one of the largest of its kind in North America. He also is founder and president of the Metta Center for Nonviolence and the author of *Our Spiritual Crisis* and *The Search for a Nonviolent Future*, which received a 2002 American Book Award and has been translated into several languages. His writing has appeared in *The Wall Street Journal* and elsewhere and he has spoken and written about nonviolence, meditation, and world peace for more than thirty years. He is chairman of the board of PeaceWorkers and was among the early founders of Nonviolent Peaceforce, now a global nonviolent peacekeeping service that has operated or is at work in Mindanao, Sri Lanka, South Sudan, and many other dangerous locales to "protect human life and promote human rights" as an impartial third party committed to nonviolent methods.

Michael's main work today, however, is with the Metta Center for Nonviolence, which he cofounded in 1982. Metta produces books, films, blog posts, and other materials as well as developing and maintaining the Roadmap model for an integrated nonviolent strategy, conducting retreats, and taking to the airwaves with *Peace Paradigm Radio*, broadcasting biweekly from KWMR in Point Reyes, California.

Among other awards, Michael received the 2007 Jamnalal Bajaj International Award for Promoting Gandhian Values Outside India.

Michael is a student of Sri Eknath Easwaran, founder of the Blue Mountain Center of Meditation (easwaran.org). He has lived at the center's ashram in Marin County since 1970 and is a presenter for their programs of passage meditation.

METTA CENTER *for* **NONVIOLENCE**

About Metta

Headquartered in Petaluma, California, the Metta Center for Nonviolence is a nonprofit dedicated to promoting nonviolence worldwide. The center was founded in 1982 by students of Sri Eknath Easwaran, founder of the Blue Mountain Center of Meditation.

Metta, dubbed a "small by mighty" organization by some, works on many fronts and many levels to carry out its nonviolent mission. Metta is a resource for activists, educators, the media, and anyone interested in learning more about "the greatest power humanity has been endowed with." On board are research fellows, interns, and volunteers as well as staff, working on (among other things) a grand strategy called Roadmap that can bring many ongoing projects into a cohesive, strategic trajectory along Gandhian lines. Metta has consulted in India with former heads and members of the Shanti Sena ("Peace Army"), instigated by Gandhi. Metta hosts a biweekly radio program, *Peace Paradigm Radio*, and has produced training films originally made for the United Nations.

All of these projects aim to help people use nonviolence safely and effectively. Gandhi experimented with principled nonviolence in literally every walk of life, from health care to national defense, for it has the potential ultimately to change human culture so that unwanted regimes and injustice are not only dislodged but permanently denied a grip on societies. It can be used to good effect by anyone who understands its basic principles, with the ultimate potential to create a nonviolent world.

Facilitating that great change is Metta's work. Learn more about us at mettacenter.org.

Berrett–Koehler
BK Publishers

Berrett-Koehler is an independent publisher dedicated to an ambitious mission: *Creating a World That Works for All.*

We believe that to truly create a better world, action is needed at all levels—individual, organizational, and societal. At the individual level, our publications help people align their lives with their values and with their aspirations for a better world. At the organizational level, our publications promote progressive leadership and management practices, socially responsible approaches to business, and humane and effective organizations. At the societal level, our publications advance social and economic justice, shared prosperity, sustainability, and new solutions to national and global issues.

A major theme of our publications is "Opening Up New Space." Berrett-Koehler titles challenge conventional thinking, introduce new ideas, and foster positive change. Their common quest is changing the underlying beliefs, mindsets, institutions, and structures that keep generating the same cycles of problems, no matter who our leaders are or what improvement programs we adopt.

We strive to practice what we preach—to operate our publishing company in line with the ideas in our books. At the core of our approach is stewardship, which we define as a deep sense of responsibility to administer the company for the benefit of all of our "stakeholder" groups: authors, customers, employees, investors, service providers, and the communities and environment around us.

We are grateful to the thousands of readers, authors, and other friends of the company who consider themselves to be part of the "BK Community." We hope that you, too, will join us in our mission.

A BK Currents Book

This book is part of our BK Currents series. BK Currents books advance social and economic justice by exploring the critical intersections between business and society. Offering a unique combination of thoughtful analysis and progressive alternatives, BK Currents books promote positive change at the national and global levels. To find out more, visit **www.bkconnection.com**.

Berrett–Koehler
Publishers

A community dedicated to creating
a world that works for all

Dear Reader,

Thank you for picking up this book and joining our worldwide community of Berrett-Koehler readers. We share ideas that bring positive change into people's lives, organizations, and society.

To welcome you, we'd like to offer you a free e-book. You can pick from among twelve of our bestselling books by entering the promotional code **BKP92E** here: http://www.bkconnection.com/welcome.

When you claim your free e-book, we'll also send you a copy of our e-newsletter, the *BK Communiqué*. Although you're free to unsubscribe, there are many benefits to sticking around. In every issue of our newsletter you'll find

- A free e-book
- Tips from famous authors
- Discounts on spotlight titles
- Hilarious insider publishing news
- A chance to win a prize for answering a riddle

Best of all, our readers tell us, "Your newsletter is the only one I actually read." So claim your gift today, and please stay in touch!

Sincerely,

Charlotte Ashlock
Steward of the BK Website

Questions? Comments? Contact me at bkcommunity@bkpub.com.

MIX
From responsible
sources
FSC® C113845
www.fsc.org

Certified

Corporation
bcorporation.net